Counselling Made Simple

A Beginner's Guide To Understanding The Practice
Of A Professional Counsellor

Sola & Nike Ajayi

ISBN: 978-978-993-799-8

Cover Design & Layout: Oluwatobi Adesanya

Published by:
 Heart2World Publishing
heart2worldpublishing.org
heart2worldpublishing@gmail.com
30, Muyiwa Opaleye. Surulere

For information on distribution, translation, or bulk sales,
please contact
Sola Ajayi
+2348023415303, 08023415645
therealmtribe@gmail.com

Dedication

This book is dedicated to God; the author of life. He is the one who inspires us and keeps us going.

Acknowledgment

Writing this section of the book would be difficult because there are lots of people we would like to acknowledge for their contributions towards the success of our ministry and this book as well.

Praise Fowowe (founder of The Institute of Family Engineering and Development) your investment in our ministry and profession is unquantifiable. Thank you for being our Coach, friend, and brother for over 25 years.

Reverend Dr and Reverend Mrs Vic and May Victor, founders of The Institute of Marriage and Family Affairs; thank you for your investment in us. We are profoundly grateful.

To Pastor Ajisola; thank you for giving us wings to fly and giving us your immense support and fatherly blessings. We can't thank you enough.

Pastor Peter Adedeji and Pastor Yemi Lebi; thank you for your prayers, encouragement and support.

To our own special mentee and writer, Oluwatobiloba Adesanya, thank you for spurring us to write this. For your tirelessness, sleepless nights, and unwavering faith in us. You are a major answer to our prayers.

I celebrate every member of the REALM Tribe and those who have been a part of our success story.

To everyone who we have been privileged to lead, pastor, and mentor, we celebrate you and we thank you for believing in us. We look forward to more of your success stories.

Foreword

Sola & Nike Ajayi, a couple I have come to love and cherish for many years now; have written this amazing book which is a reflection of their experience and passion for people.

Since I came in contact with them while I served as Provincial Pastor RCCG Province 7 (Lagos State) their desire and passion to help and build people has not abated.

As a Pastor and leader myself, I've had to step in to resolve many issues with individuals, friends, families, or groups, so I know how impactful counselling can be in bringing change, growth and progress.

In this book, the authors have penned down thoughts to help you learn the basics of becoming a professional counsellor.

This is one book you'll read again and again.

Pastor Ayo Ajisola
Pastor in Charge of Province
RCCG FCT 5, ABUJA

CONTENT

 Nothing is impossible for those
who act after wise counsel and
careful thought.

Introduction

Where there is no counsel, the people fall; But
in the multitude of counselors there is safety.
- Proverbs 11:14

Counsel is just like oxygen; we need it to survive and thrive. Attempting to live life without some sort of guidance could lead to death; maybe not in the literal sense, but relationships could die, career dreams could be cut short, marriages could break up, and your mental health may suffer.

We believe a healthy dose of counsel regarding the matters of life – business, career, family life, relationships, sex – minimizes mistakes and increases our chances of achieving success. As a matter of fact, this book in your hands is a product of the counsel, advice, and encouragement we received to start writing.

Counselling is a practice we've come to love; together with a repertoire of skills and competencies we've built over the years, we've seen immense results in the lives of the hundreds of individuals we've been privileged to work with.

It was in the midst of one of our counselling sessions with a couple preparing for marriage that we had a light bulb moment. We realized that this practice which we do so effortlessly may not come so easily for others. So, we got to work immediately. We created time and space to deliberately work on taking our years of knowledge and practice and distilling into writing so that you can find this useful for your own practice as a counsellor. This book is the first of many to come.

You may be asking, 'With the load of information available and several online learning platforms, do people still need to hire a counsellor, sit with a therapist or even read a book?" The answer is a BIG YES! By now, you will agree that information alone does not guarantee transformation. There is a lacuna between the two that can only be filled by having informed and well-trained counsellors, teachers, mentors to teach and guide individuals in their respective paths.

This book is by no means a succinct exploration of counselling as a practice, but it will serve as a foundation for you, and more importantly launch you on a quest to becoming better at helping and impacting the lives of people through your knowledge.

With that said, we invite you to come along with us on this journey.

Sola & Nike Ajayi.
Lagos, 2021.

What is Counselling

01

The word 'counsel' stems from an Old French word 'conseiller' which means to advise, counsel. It also has a Latin variation 'consiliari' which means to plan, offer an opinion. If you have ever had to ask someone for an opinion; be it a parent, teacher, pastor, or mentor, what you received from them is counsel. Putting the two derivatives together, we infer that a counsellor advises, helps people make better plans or form better opinions about something or about a course of action.

According to The Counsellor's Guide UK, counselling refers to "the generic name given to a supportive service that provides individuals with guidance and help to understand, accept and overcome emotional issues, problems and concerns, some of which may be long-standing."

We believe if you're reading this, you must have an interest in helping people, guiding people and helping them make better decisions regarding their specific area of need. You may have at certain points in your life received the care and guidance of a counsellor which helped you make better decisions. Or, perhaps, you didn't have the privilege of good counsel and now want to help others. Whatever divide you fall in, you are welcome to explore the path. Before going further, let's establish what counselling is NOT.

What counselling is not

Having an understanding of what counselling is NOT helps to narrow down and gain better insight as to what counselling really is and you can get started on that journey to becoming a professional counsellor.

1. Counselling is not JUDGING or CONDEMNING people:

Many people have resolved to die in silence simply because others judged them wrongly or harshly after they shared their heart burdens with them. Judging and condemning people is not in the toolbox of a professional counsellor.

Counselling has nothing to do with judging or condemning people.

When people muster the courage to open up — something lots of people find very difficult to do – the least a counsellor should do is to commend and celebrate their courage.

Opening up to the right person should be the first step to healing, clarity and direction for anyone seeking counsel. Contrary to what people believe, judging and condemning people doesn't make them better. It makes them curl up more into their shell and vow never to seek for help again. Counsellors don't shut people up; they help them up. Later on in this book, we would share some of the critical skills you must have in your toolbox as a professional counsellor.

2. Counselling is not a MAGIC WAND:

If you've ever travelled via any public transport in certain locations, you most likely would have come across certain persons claiming to be 'Doctors' offering some kind of medicine that cures literally all the diseases in the world. With so much confidence and with a puffed-up chest, they make unverifiable claims about their products; and people are swayed into buying these products. You must not approach counselling this way. Everyone is wired differently. We all have unique upbringing, beliefs, experiences, values, knowledge and exposure that have shaped our lives. One counselling session with someone will most likely not solve the problem.

When working with an individual, it is important to lay the cards on the table that it requires their cooperation, openness, and willingness to make a change, for change to really happen in their lives. Change will not happen overnight, but over time.

Counselling is not an instant solution or the magical cure. It majorly provides the opportunity to gain better insight to whatever the situation is and it increases the possibility of coming up with viable solutions and actions steps. More so, counselling becomes effective when the person seeking it is willing. They must demonstrate the willingness to change, make adjustments and take better actions. No matter how much of an expert a Doctor or a Lawyer is, if the persons they are attending to is unwilling, there would be no results.

3. Counselling is not advice-giving.

The counsellor is not to act or present him/herself as a superior to the person being counselled. Rather, the counsellor guides the individual towards a solution that works with them. Counselling is not giving advice or prescribing a solution in the way a doctor prepares prescription drugs. The counsellor is not to impose perspectives or ideas. Doing that makes the person dependent on you as the counsellor. You must strive to guide people till the solution originates from them such that they can take independent actions based on your guidance.

4. Counselling is not a one-sided conversation.

What does this mean? Let's use these two scenarios.

Imagine a man; let's call him Jack, walks through the door of your office as a counsellor and sits down to have a session with you, and just right after exchanging pleasantries, proceeds to share about all the terrible things in his life and how things aren't working well and why he needs help. All the while he talks while giving you no space to talk, ask more leading questions or to understand him better. How would such a conversation be fruitful or helpful to both parties? There would be zero results. It goes the other way round too. It shouldn't be just the counsellor offering advice or giving tips and sharing 1001 examples of other people. No. Counselling is an ongoing conversation that must be between the counsellor and the individual being counselled.

To put it simply, counselling is a compound word that encompasses the many different kinds of therapy and therapeutic aspects that exist. Counsellors typically help people understand their situations, unravel new paradigms, and evolve solutions to change or improve their current situations.

Are you interested in helping people, being a tour

guide for them as they navigate various aspects of their lives?

If   YES, you are welcome to join me in the next chapter.

Flip the page…

Types Of Counselling

02

In the previous chapter, we mentioned that counselling is an umbrella word for several forms of counselling and therapy. That means there are different fields. For the purpose of this book, we would limit it to the area of Family-Life Counselling – this is the field we have chosen to major on.

The fields under Family Life Counselling includes (but not limited to):

- Pre-marital counselling
- Post-marital counselling
- Matchmaking counselling
- Parenting counselling
- Sex counselling and therapy
- Family systems
- Blended family counselling
- Grief counselling.

With our over 15 years of practice, we've found ourselves in all of these fields as we worked with individuals prepare for marriage and to resolve issues in their marriage. We must say here that our experience with people have been different. As different as our faces and fingerprints are, even so are the trauma, phobia, beliefs, values, and life situations of people different.

Pre-marital counselling involves two individuals who have made a decision to get married, coming together to seek guidance, insight, and clarity regarding their marital decision. The choice of a life partner is one of the most life-altering decisions anyone can make. Making a marital decision all alone without quality input from others may not augur well no matter how much in love the couple may be.

A statistic from 2006 revealed that 50% of people marrying could end up in divorce. 40% of first marriages could end up in divorce. 60% of second marriages could end up in divorce and 70% of third marriages could end up in divorce. That same statistics revealed that marital preparations could reduce divorce rate by 30%.

Studies also show that a couple is likely to have improved marital experiences by 79% better than those who had no form of premarital preparations.

These statistics speak for themselves; they need no further explanation. Weddings are conducted weekly and people take that life-defining oath and put pen to paper as they say 'Yes, I do' but only a few of them know what they are really doing. This is why pre-marital counselling will always be relevant. It is a type of counselling and we've established a full practice in this. This is also one of the major services we offer at REALM (Relationship Essentials And Life Matters).

Pre-marital counselling helps singles prepare for marriage. It helps couples have a strong and healthy relationship as they head into marriage. It helps them identify areas of weaknesses and other aspects of their lives that could pose a critical problem to the marriage in the future of the marriage. Generally, pre-marital counselling covers areas such as finance, communication, temperament difference, decision making, belief and values, sex, marital roles, the desire to have children; to mention a few.

Post-marital counselling: while pre-marital counselling is almost a fad and common place – though some couples do not go through this process (this is NOT recommended), post-marital counselling is often not talked about. Couples only seek counsel or help whenever their marriage is already hitting the rocks or have hit the rocks.

If quality counselling and therapeutic intervention was critical in the formation process of the marriage, it follows that it will also be helpful in the marriage. We've heard from new couples who feel all alone and abandoned after they've walked down the aisle. It often appears like all the counselling only prepared them to 'start' and not for the long stretch ahead. Marriage is actually not a sprint; it is a lifetime commitment. Marital Counselling must be approached in the same way we maintain a working relationship and schedule visits with family doctors. . Reports show that more than 70% of health issues we face stem from emotional problems[1]. If counselling is taken seriously, good health will not be far fetched.

[1] Journal of Epidemiology and Community Health 1997

Match making counselling: some persons consider themselves unlucky when it comes to making the right marital choices. This could be due to their experiences growing up and other stories they've heard. On the other hand, there are those who have clarity about the kind of marriage they want, the values they desire in their partner and the vision they have for their future. While these people have clarity, they are not able to find or 'see' their partner. This is where matchmaking counselling comes in.

A biblical story of the man called Blind Bartimaeus comes to mind here. Bartmaeus was a man who had clarity. He knew what he really wanted. He was self-aware and well-informed. Though he didn't have sight, he knew Jesus, though. He acquainted himself with information on the person that could help him.

Scripture says; *"Then they came to Jericho. As Jesus and his disciples, together with a large crowd, were leaving the city, a blind man, Bartimaeus (which means "son of Timaeus"), was sitting by the roadside begging. 47 When he heard that it was Jesus of Nazareth, he began to shout, "Jesus, Son of David, have mercy on me!" (Mark 10:46-47).*

Even when people tried to shut him up, he shouted the more. It shows that he was persistent and relentless in the pursuit of his goal.

When Jesus met him he asked, "What do you want me to do for you?" Bartimaeus had only one request, "Rabbi, I want to see." His request was granted. The insight here is that most singles are well-informed, they've read books attended conferences, etc.; they know what they want. They never feel discouraged even when people say things like, "Your standards are too high. Will you ever find a man/woman like that?" Individuals like these need guidance to 'see' their desired partner. Jesus, in this story was like the matchmaker. He 'matched' Bartimaeus with sight. Matchmakers are connectors.

Typically, matchmaking counselling involves the counsellor meeting up with select individuals, interviewing them, sharing dating advice, and basically getting them ready to meet their potential spouse. This is done independently. The matchmaking counsellor connects the dots after careful evaluation, personality tests/evaluation, love language, belief/culture compatibility test, faith based evaluation, and other background checks have been made.

Parenting counselling: children are gifts from God. Couples in marriage (though not all) desire, at some point, to conceive and raise their children in the comfort of their home.

Becoming a parent is life-changing. Parents come to love, care, nurture and nourish in a way they never did before. However, in many ways, parents raise their kids in the very same way they were raised without considering that the times have changed.

Parenting counselling helps to prepare parents to raise their kids properly. It is a type of counselling that provides parents with the knowledge, guidance, techniques to navigate through this life-changing moment in their marriage. Parenting can be overwhelming if not properly prepared for, this is where parenting counselling helps. Parenting counselling is needed at critical stages of life; for example: new parents or parents with special children. Parenting a teenager is different from raising an infant.

Counselling helps parents navigate all the phases of their parenting journey successfully.

Sex counselling & Therapy: according to Healthline, sex therapy is "a type of talk therapy that's designed to help individuals and couples address medical, psychological, personal, or interpersonal factors impacting sexual satisfaction."

Sex counselling helps to resolve issues such as erectile dysfunction, low libido, lack of response to sexual stimuli, low confidence, inability to reach orgasm, distressing sexual thoughts; just to mention a few.

Family systems Counselling: the family bond is second to none. However, families still have issues to resolve. There are conflicts that arise within families that take years to resolve, and some never get resolved.

Family systems counselling/therapy is that form of counselling that supports people in resolving conflict with family members or problems that exist within a family. This form of therapy helps families to communicate better, understand one another, and to resolve conflict more quickly.

Blended Family Counselling: this kind of counselling is for step families, single parents or widows who intend to get married again. In situations where someone loses their significant other (especially after having kids), there is a need for such families to blend again when the person remarries and starts another family with someone else. This kind of counselling helps to bridge the gap and help the new family integrate easily.

Grief counselling: Grief is an inevitable part of life. It is something we'll experience at a point in our life's journey. Grief counselling is also called bereavement counselling. It is specially designed to help individuals cope with the loss of a loved one.

Typically, a grief counsellor helps to develop methods to handle the grief. Most importantly, it provides people an outlet to express their deepest emotions and feelings.

In grief counselling, there are stages of grief which the counsellor has to walk with the client thorough. It is not an instant thing, it takes time, patience, and effort to work with clients that are grieving.

GETTING *Started*

03

I f you've read this far, then we're convinced that you really desire to become a professional counsellor.

It all starts with:

Learning: Just as with every practice, there is a learning curve. While certain people are empathetic and have the knack for helping people, there is a need to further study, get trained, and certified in the practice of being a counsellor. The passion you have to help people should drive you to know more and be more. The better you become, the more resourceful and helpful you would be.

It's been over 15 years of practice as counsellors and yet we keep on learning more. We recently gained admission to pursue a masters in Psychology. We've seen the need to learn and equip ourselves for what is to come. The business of helping people requires that you first invest in yourself, develop your skill set, and make the required human connections with other experts in the field.

Gain the trust of people: People are in layers; we keep our deepest thoughts, feelings and emotions away from people. It takes a certain level of feeling safe for people to open at all.

As a counsellor, you have to create that environment of safety and trust so that people can come to you and also feel free to share their burdens in the most honest way possible. It does you and the client no good when there is no openness.

Creating that safe place requires that you connect with them; find common ground and build up casual conversations with them. Ask about their family, hobbies, work, life, business, and the things that interest them.

People relate with those they know, like and trust. You

have to build that into every conversation from the start. Have conversation 'ice-breakers' at your fingertips. In other words, have tips and techniques you can use to get people talking and sharing freely.

Confidentiality: the advent of media has helped us a great deal, but it has also broken a lot of people emotionally. Almost daily, we see private conversations screenshotted and shared online, confidential information is shared so freely for people to share their opinions – opinions that the persons in question never asked for; etc. These should not be the case with a professional counsellor. Establish before hand with clients that you will not share details of their private conversation publicly. Confidentiality is key! However, if there is a need to share their stories for others to glean from their experience, ensure to get the express and documented permission of the client. If the permission is granted, the story must be shared in an anonymous manner. The person (s) listening to the story should not have a clue as to 'who' the person is. The most important thing is the lesson to be learned.

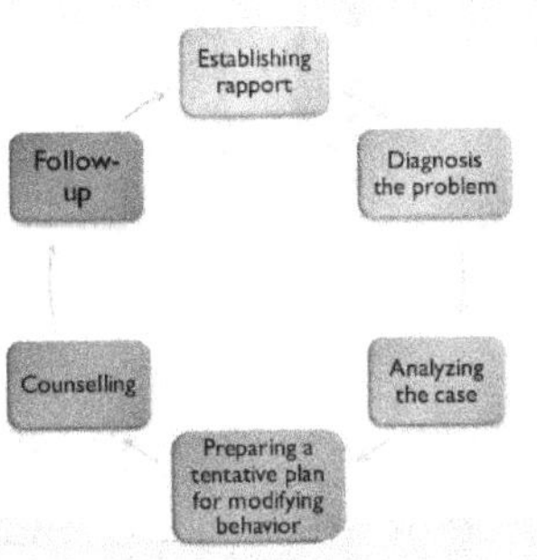

TOOLS OF
A
Counsellor

04

Courses, trainings, and certifications are important to develop competence as a counsellor. However, there are many other skills we'll consider soft skills which you must deploy over and over again in your practice. We really can't stress enough how vital these tools are in understanding people and helping you be of help to those you come across in your practice.

1. Listen: Most people listen, not to understand, but to respond. This is why people complete sentences for others just before they finish.

Really, as a counsellor you have to do better. To truly listen, it requires your full attention, focus, to unearth what is not even said in the conversation. Listening is always on two levels, but there are actually three levels. Namely; listening for what is being said, listening to what is not being said, and listening to what they are finding difficult to voice out. It takes active, not passive, listening to understand the details of the narrative or stories people share with you.

Like Stephen R. Covey wrote, "Most people do not listen with the intent to understand; they listen with the intent to reply. They're either speaking or preparing to speak."

When you're really listening, the individual you're attending to can easily know. Listening comes with empathy, eye-contact, follow-up questions, building rapport, and even occasional silence.

For example, if a woman is sharing her experience with a husband that speaks ill of her, never compliments or praises her efforts, as a counsellor, demonstrate empathy and allow her go on with her narration. At certain points where the client pauses and they are unable to find their words, help them paraphrase what you have heard them say.

For example:

Client Victoria: "My husband beats me at every chance he gets. He doesn't even care if the kids are watching or our neighbors hear my screams. I really can't take this anymore. See my scars, I am a shadow of myself."

Counsellor Adenike: "This must be really difficult for you. You are concerned about not just yourself, but your kids and even others around you. How does this make you feel?"

Carrying on the conversation in this manner, no doubt, helps to keep the conversation going. But it all starts from listening to understand rather than to reply.

2. Questions: Questions are your best friend. You must know how to use them with your clients. That's where the conversation starts.

Questions direct the flow of your time with your counselee and is the key to unlocking everything you need to know.

How well you ask the questions determine how helpful your sessions would be. As much as possible, use open-ended questions when speaking with people.

You know why? Open-ended questions get people talking. Close-ended questions only restrict people to controlled or one-word responses. For example:

- Close ended question: Will you marry him?

- Open-ended question: Why do you want to get married to him?

- Close ended question: Are you sad today?

- Open ended question: How are you really feeling today?

The quality of questions you ask determines the quality of responses you receive.

Questions are so important because they open up new areas for conversation. While someone is talking, they may stumble on something they weren't even thinking about before or even thought to share before the conversation began.

As a counsellor, you must be prompt to respond to those talking points and ask more questions if need be. For instance, a woman in a marriage where she feels unloved may start by saying something like; "I've been married for 5 years and I must say that the only time I ever felt loved was just the first 6 months of our marriage. It feels like after that 'honeymoon phase' as they call it, he just switched off. Yes, he isn't unfaithful or seeing other women. But I just don't know why. He once told me that he doesn't like his job and doesn't feel fulfilled but he works so hard and makes the family financially okay. I really don't know what the problem is."

Can you notice new talking points here?

As a counsellor, you should spot the area where she said, "After 6 months in the marriage" "He once told me he doesn't feel fulfilled at work"

These two areas call for more inquiry as to why that is. As you continue to probe, the person will open up more details about their story that will help arrive a meaningful conclusion or answer.

The easy path to asking the right questions is to ask the 5W1H questions: Who? What? Where? When? Why? How? Ask questions with these words. It helps to stir the conversation forward.

3. Empathy:

There is nothing as beautiful and heart-warming as being understood by another human being. Humans are naturally prone to judge other people and make them feel less of themselves especially when those people have erred or messed up in one way or the other.

Get this: as a counsellor you will be dealing with people who have messed up, are being messed up, or have messed other people up. By 'mess up' we mean people who have been hurt, are hurting or even are themselves hurting others. Since people fall into any of these three categories, you must learn to empathize and not to criticize them.

Empathy refers to that ability to feel or share the emotions of someone else. It's that ability to understand and feel the aspirations, conflicts, weaknesses, and pains of other persons while still knowing and feeling your own.

Empathy is a skill you must be build as a counsellor. Some persons are naturally gifted at this; they just know how to feel what others feel. And people often know this through their body language, disposition, and their words as well. In cases where you might want to shed a tear, it is advisable to excuse yourself. Being overly emotional may alter the entire process of the counselling. For instance, if you are resolving a dispute between a couple and along the way you begin to tear up when the man or the woman share their side of the story, this may communicate that you are going to take sides with the person. As professional counsellors, we have been taught to excuse ourselves (if need be) so as to calm down and maintain a neutral state. We must say here that empathy is not the same as sympathy. Sympathy means caring for someone who is going through a very tough time or is grieving over a loss or something tragic that may have happened. A person can sympathize or care for someone without feeling deeply what the person is feeling. Empathy produces something inside you: the desire to HELP.

According to US National Library of Medicine National Institutes of Health there are two types of empathy: Cognitive and Affective empathy. Cognitive empathy has to do with identifying and understanding emotions in other people. On the other hand, affective empathy refers to the ability to feel the emotions that other people feel as well.

4. The God- factor: our experiences as faith-based counsellors reveals that one must never joke with the God factor. Our prayer of faith, declaring positive results before the manifestation of the result is pivotal. There is a realm where knowledge and all that you have known will become ineffective. But as you take a stand in prayer, God begins to give directions and insights you never knew. Despite the fact that we invest in knowledge, we've developed a lot of techniques and curated knowledge that was totally divinely inspired. Being a faith-based counsellor takes you one step higher and gives you divine ability to help your clients find a head way.

The Ripple Effect of Counselling

05

In this chapter, the focus would be on the ripple effect counselling has on people. When you work with one individual, it affects others in their circle.

Here is a feedback we received..

"I was in the congregation one evening during a Youth Convention when Pastor Nike Ajayi mounted the altar and ministered on relationship and marriage.

Her words were weighty, deeper than the surface, yet very relatable. I also watched her husband Pastor Sola Ajayi (Provincial Youth Pastor) seated, listening intently to what his wife was teaching. It was such a sight to behold. I knew instantly that I was in the presence of not only an anointed woman, but a professional who knew how to function in both capacities to bring help to people she came across. Pastor Sola and Nike's marriage is a model and a whole course for us all to learn.

Later on, as marriage seemed like it was coming closer for me, I decided that she was going to be our Marriage Counsellor. I had no doubt in my heart that this would have a tremendous impact on my own journey and that of my fiancée. During one of our meetings, she shared and demonstrated a role play she developed for married couples and how it helped couples understand themselves better.

What was this special technique? I can assure you that it isn't something you'll read in a book or find on Google. It must have been divinely inspired; just maybe.

She said, "In a couple's workshop, I asked couples to exchange one leg of their shoes. Then,

I asked them to attempt to walk with one leg of their shoe and other leg with one of their spouse's shoe."

Being a very imaginative person, I could not contain my amazement. "That's uncomfortable" I thought. It truly was. Imagine (as a man) putting on one leg of your shoe and having on a 5-inch heel on your right leg, how would you move, walk, or even run?

She continued, "In that session, I saw the couples breakdown and begin to cry as the meaning of the exercise dawned on them."

She drove home a point that day and it stuck with me. But little did I know that I would administer the same therapy to another couple who have been over 23 years in marriage – my parents.

I met them one evening and I realized they were having quite an argument. Apparently, it had become a norm for Mom to complain about a lot of things while not acknowledging any of the good things that Dad was doing to make her happy or make the home better. She obviously was working hard and still building her career and believed that she deserved some credit too. Dad on the other hand felt mom's own concerns and challenges at work were irrelevant or not as important as his own and felt that she never appreciated him enough.

Like a referee, I listened to both sides of the story. I should say here that I love my parents so dearly; in fact, I call them my heroes. They never fail to amaze me; the story of their marriage is one that inspires me every day.

The words that began to flow from me that evening made them keep quiet, at least temporarily. They had never heard me speak in such a manner before. I shared with them the impact of nature/nurture on their marriage. I asked if they knew the love language of one another. I was also able to help them see how the peculiarities of their upbringing made them act the way they did.

It was then I realized my interactions with

Pastor Sola & Nike Ajayi and the things they taught me were having a profound effect on my understanding of people and my overall outlook about life.

Just as I was about round off, like a light bulb, the couple exercise she talked about came to mind. I immediately asked Dad and Mom to get a pair of their shoes. Each one exchanged one leg while putting on the other. I then asked them to try to walk in the shoes. Mom hadn't taken up to three steps before she began to tear up.

My dad who rarely shows emotions was so emotional and close to tears that very night. He tried masking his emotions by letting out occasional sighs and deep breathing, but he really couldn't conceal it. In the end, that night, I saw reconciliation. That exercise made him 'see' what Mom had been saying all the while.

The exercise also made Mom 'see' what Dad was saying and the adjustments she needed to make. They each saw the need to empathize, understand and celebrate one another. That night, their friendship was restored and their conversations came back alive. It's been a long time now, and their love and bond just keeps on growing every day.

Sesan Emmanuel

When I received this feedback from Sesan, it struck a chord in my heart and I concluded that if people would open up to counselling and therapy, the effect goes beyond the individual. It affects their own relationships, career, marriage, and even the marriage of other people.

As a counsellor, your work transcends that one individual you are working with. It extends to tens, hundreds, and even thousands of other people that one person will come in contact with in the future.

I've shared this one story to help you see how your own efforts in your corner of the world makes a world of difference elsewhere. I was only speaking with Sesan, I didn't know that the lessons he was learning would prove to be so impactful for his own parents as well. You may be working with a child, a parent, a mother, a couple; at all times, keep in mind that their lives will impact others out there.

Self-care is Non-negotiable

06

The joy of helping people resolve issues keep us going all the time. Guiding people in their choices, decisions, and helping them become better as a result, is one of the dividends of toeing this line of work. However, this could also create an illusion, or a perception that as counsellors we ourselves are invincible.

The toxic situations counsellors have to handle from time to time exposes them directly to the trauma and pain that others are going through. Is there really an immunity against this? Can our mental health really go unaffected by the issues we are exposed to?

This is why I've saved this chapter for the last. Self-care is non-negotiable in your practice.

Socrates, the ancient philosopher, said, "Man, know thyself." Another philosopher said, "To thyself be true." You have to know your limits, know when to take a break to replenish yourself, go on a vacation and just to 'clear your head.'

15 years of practice has taught us the need to constantly refill ourselves, clear our schedule and go on a break. There will always be issues to resolve, but without proper self-care, you may not be healthy enough to help more people. Again, it is important to note that not all cases actually end up positive. Sometimes, after frantic efforts to save a marriage, it still collapses. After efforts to prepare singles for marriage, they end up breaking up and going their separate ways.

Life isn't linear. With certain persons, we've had to terminate the sessions with them because we couldn't see willingness on their part to change and to resolve the challenges they had. Knowing when to discontinue working with certain persons is also a form of self-care. Don't get drained trying to help unwilling people.

For every one that is unwilling to make use of the benefits of counselling, there are countless others desiring to have you in their homes and their lives.

You cannot afford to burn out or reach the point of exhaustion. The Merriam-Webster's Online Dictionary defines burnout as exhaustion of physical or emotional strength or motivation usually as a result of prolonged stress or frustration. Don't be a victim.

How do you prevent a burnout and really care for yourself

1. *Be easy on yourself.* Realize that you are not a superman. Be gentle. Design a work schedule you are comfortable with and stick to it.

2. *Have a support group.* This support group could be friends in the same industry you can connect with and share experiences. Interacting with others provides emotional support for you and helps you know that you are not alone.

3. *Leverage on your mentors.* Mentors help to provide insight, balance, and redirection.

4. Laugh. Play. Practice gratitude daily.

5. Learn to say NO.

6. Block out time to rest, exercise, and go on breaks.

About the authors

Sola & Nike Ajayi are trained Family Life Practitioners, intentional parents, pastors and entrepreneurs of repute.

They are the Pastors in charge of Zone in RCCG and also double as Provincial Youth Pastors, presiding over youths in 120 parishes in the province.

They are certified members and trainers in the following family Life Organisations:

1. The Institute of Family Engineering & Development, Nigeria.

2. The Rising Oaks Ministry, Canada.

3. The Institute of Marriage and Family Affairs, USA

4. The RCCG, National Family Affairs Unit.

5. Haggai International Institute for Advanced Leadership Training.

6. Emotions City

They founded **REALM** (Relationship Essentials and Life Matters). REALM warehouses these three groups: THE-POST WEDDING COUNSELLOR, THE SINGLES' HAVEN and THE MARRIAGE MATCH MINDER.

The love, ministry and vision for marriages and Homes started when they were both at the University of Ado - Ekiti, when God told them on the first day of their courtship that their home will be a role model for other homes.

Sola and Nike Ajayi are gloriously married for seventeen years, they are blessed with three world changers.